Grade
K

Read and Learn

With Classic Stories

**McGraw-Hill
Children's Publishing**

Columbus, Ohio

Acknowledgments

McGraw-Hill Children's Publishing Editorial/Art & Design Team

Vincent F. Douglas, *President*
Tracey E. Dils, *Publisher*
Phyllis Armelie Sibbing, B.S. Ed., *Project Editor*
Andrea Pelleschi, *Story Editor*
Rose Audette, *Art Director*
Jennifer Bowers, *Interior Layout Design and Production*
Nancy Allton, *Interior Layout Production*

Also Thanks to:

Roxanna Marino Knapp, *Story Reteller*
Edith Reynolds, M.S. Ed., *Editor*
Nancy Holt Johnson, B.S. Ed., *Editor*
Wendy Rassmussen, *Cover Illustration*
  Story Illustrations:
    CD Hullinger, *Mother Goose Rhymes*
    Laura J. Bryant, *Goldilocks and the Three Bears*
    Douglas A Bowles, *The Gingerbread Man*
    Tammie Lyon, *Little Red Riding Hood*
    Horatio Elena, *The Three Little Pigs*
    Ilene Richards, *The Three Billy Goats Gruff*
  Activity Illustrations:
    Burgandy Beam, *Mother Goose Rhymes*
    Linda Howard Bittner, *Goldilocks and the Three Bears*
    Douglas A. Bowles, *The Gingerbread Man*
    Tammie Lyon, *Little Red Riding Hood*
    Horatio Elena, *The Three Little Pigs*
    Ilene Richards, *The Three Billy Goats Gruff*

McGraw-Hill
Children's Publishing

A Division of The **McGraw·Hill** Companies

Published by American Education Publishing, an imprint of McGraw-Hill Children's Publishing
Copyright © 2002 McGraw-Hill Children's Publishing.

Send all inquires to:
McGraw-Hill Children's Publishing
8787 Orion Place
Columbus. OH 43240-4027

ISBN 1-56189-681-0

1 2 3 4 5 6 7 8 9   06 05 04 03 02 01

Table of Contents

Introduction for Parents and Teachers

The Importance of Reading Classic Tales

Storytelling is an art that started long before stories were recorded and published. Orally passed from storyteller to storyteller in front of a crackling fire, many stories changed form, yet maintained similar plots and themes. We may credit these tales to names such as Jacob and Wilhelm Grimm, Charles Perrault, Joseph Jacobs, and Jørgensen and Moe, but in fact, these storytellers collected century-old stories from oral sources, crafted them, and wrote them down in the form we now enjoy.

Classic fairy tales and folk tales around the world are similar in their themes of good versus evil and intelligence or cleverness versus force or might. The details of the stories may change, but the themes remain universal.

Many fairy tales contain elements or suggestions of violence, such as the threat of being eaten by giants, witches, or ferocious wolves. In part, this violent bent emerged because early fairy tales were intended primarily for an adult audience, not for children. Fairies were often cast as the rich and powerful, with the main human character representing the poor, oppressed common person. The tales served as beacons of hope for the underprivileged in ancient times when there was little chance for social mobility.

Many psychologists today believe that fairy tales are good for children, because these tales represent what all people fear and desire, and thus help children face their own fears and wishes. Other psychologists say that children benefit from hearing stories with some element of danger, and then being reassured with happy endings in which the small, apparently powerless hero or heroine triumphs after all. This is especially true when a supportive parent takes the time to discuss the stories with his or her child and provide specific, personal reassurance.

Knowing classic stories and their characters will help ensure that your child begins to have a rich background in cultural literacy. Classic stories also expand the world of children by enriching their lives and empowering their learning. The tales present characters who undergo struggles and emerge transformed, thereby helping readers discover more about themselves. When your child identifies with these characters, he or she might better understand his or her own feelings and the feelings of other people.

Classic stories present diverse cultures, new ideas, and clever problem-solving. They use language in creative and colorful ways and serve as a springboard for your child's writing. Most of all, classic stories delight and entertain readers of all ages by providing the youngest reader with a solid base for a lifelong love of literature and reading.

About This Book

Read and Learn With Classic Stories has two main parts—the classic stories and the reading activities. The **classic stories** are a collection of rhymes, fairy tales, and folk tales. This collection may be read and reread regularly. Kindergartners and first graders will probably need some help reading the stories. Second and third graders should be able to read the stories more independently. When the book is finished, it can be saved as an anthology to begin or add to your child's home library.

Follow-up **reading activities** are included for each story to build your child's vocabulary and comprehension skills. These activities focus on skills such as phonics, word meaning, sequencing, main idea, cause and effect, and comparing and contrasting. Additional language arts activities center on grammar, punctuation, and writing. A unique feature of this book is that the activities are closely linked to the stories and not presented in isolation. They are taught within the context of the story. The benefit of this feature is a more meaningful learning experience.

Kindergartners and first graders will probably need help reading the directions, but children of this age should be able to complete the activities with a minimum of assistance. Second and third graders should be able to complete the activities more independently.

The activity pages are perforated for easy removal. There is also an **answer key** at the end of the book for immediate feedback.

A one-page **bibliography** at the end of each story is provided to guide you and your child to further reading. This list contains other tellings of the same story, usually one traditional and one with a twist, so your child can compare different approaches to the same story. Several enjoyable, age-appropriate books that are related in other ways to the story are provided as well. This list of books will come in handy during visits to the library.

A **reading skills checklist** on pages 295-296 can help you monitor your child's progress in reading comprehension. Of course, no two children progress at the same rate, but the checklist suggests appropriate reading goals for your child. Sample questions are listed for each skill. You may ask these before, during, or after reading to assess your child's ability to apply the skills.

At the end of the book you will find several pages of **everyday learning activities** you can do with your child in the subject areas of reading, math, science, social studies, and fitness and movement. These activities will extend your child's learning beyond this book.

About "Mother Goose Rhymes"

When we hear the name Mother Goose, we usually picture a sweet, grandmotherly woman wearing reading glasses, perhaps riding on the back of a goose. However, Mother Goose is actually the French scholar and storyteller Charles Perrault. In 1687, he published a book of fairy tales called *Contes de ma mère l'oye (Tales of Mother Goose)*. The French folk expression "Mother Goose tale" is similar to the expression "old wives' tale." This expression might have come about because at that time in France the teller of tales was often an old peasant woman who watched over the village geese.

In 1768, or perhaps earlier, the heirs of John Newbery, one of the first publishers of children's books, published an English version of Perrault's stories called *Mother Goose's Tales*. Then in 1781, the Newbery firm published a book of rhymes called *Mother Goose's Melody*, and the term "Mother Goose" quickly came into popular use to refer to any nursery rhymes.

Legend has it that a woman in Boston named Elizabeth Goose or Vergoose wrote the first Mother Goose rhymes, but no proof of this theory has ever been found.

Mother Goose Rhymes

Illustrated by CD Hullinger

Humpty Dumpty

Humpty Dumpty sat on a wall.
Humpty Dumpty had a great fall.

All the king's horses and all
the king's men
Couldn't put Humpty together
again!

Little Miss Muffet

Little Miss Muffet
Sat on a tuffet
Eating her curds and whey.
Along came a spider,
Who sat down beside her
And frightened
Miss Muffet away.

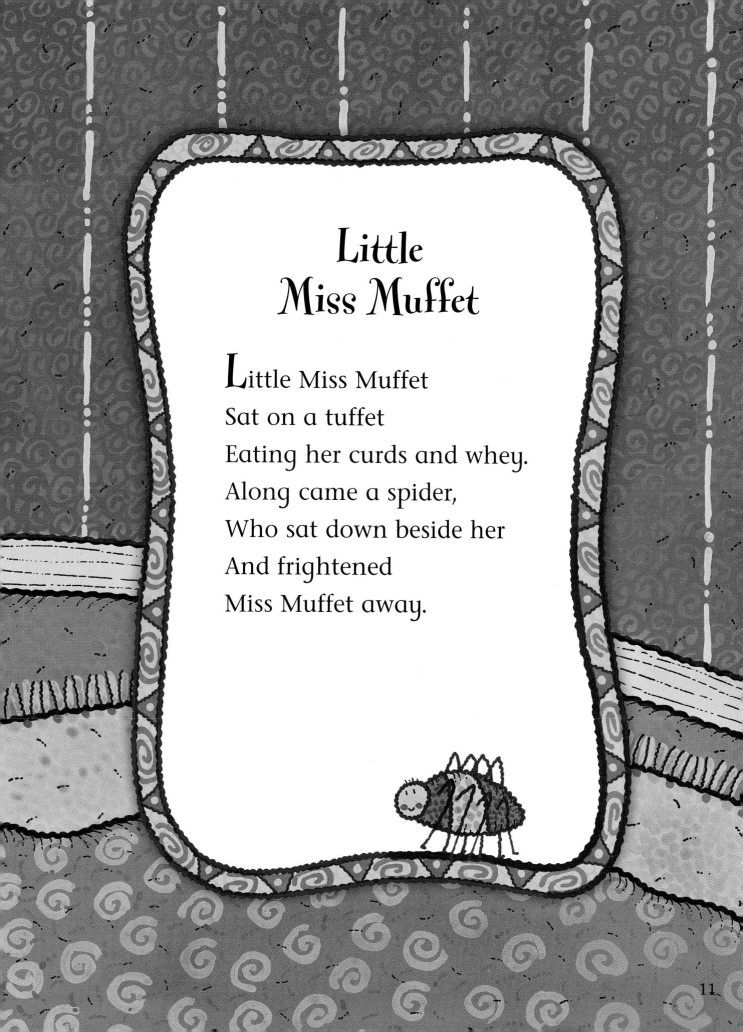

Hickory, Dickory, Dock

Hickory, dickory, dock.
The mouse ran up the clock.
The clock struck one.
The mouse ran down!
Hickory, dickory, dock.

Jack and Jill

Jack and Jill
Went up the hill
To fetch a pail of water.

Jack fell down
And broke his crown,
And Jill came tumbling after.

There Was an Old Woman

There was an old woman
who lived in a shoe.
She had so many children
She didn't know what to do.
She gave them some broth
Without any bread.
She kissed them all gently
And sent them to bed.

Peter, Peter, Pumpkin Eater

Peter, Peter, pumpkin eater,
Had a wife and couldn't keep her.
He put her in a pumpkin shell,
And there he kept her very well.

Twinkle, Twinkle, Little Star

Twinkle, twinkle, little star,
How I wonder what you are!
Up above the world so high,
Like a diamond in the sky.
Twinkle, twinkle, little star,
How I wonder what you are!

–Adapted by Jane Taylor

Baa, Baa, Black Sheep

Baa, baa, black sheep,
Have you any wool?
Yes, sir, yes, sir,
Three bags full.

One for my master,
One for my dame,
And one for the little boy
Who lives in the lane.

Baa, baa, black sheep,
Have you any wool?
Yes, sir, yes, sir,
Three bags full.

Hey, Diddle, Diddle

Hey, diddle, diddle,
The cat and the fiddle.
The cow jumped over
   the moon.
The little dog laughed
To see such sport,
And the dish ran away with
   the spoon.

To Market, To Market

To market, to market,
To buy a fat pig.
Home again, home again,
Jiggety jig.

To market, to market,
To buy a fat hog.
Home again, home again,
Jiggety jog.

Pears
50¢

Mary's Lamb

Mary had a little lamb,
Its fleece was white as snow;
And everywhere that
   Mary went,
The lamb was sure to go.

He followed her to school
   one day—
That was against the rule;
It made the children laugh
   and play
To see a lamb at school.

–Sarah Josepha Hale

Teddy Bear, Teddy Bear

Teddy bear, teddy bear,
Turn around.

Teddy bear, teddy bear,
Touch the ground.

Teddy bear, teddy bear,
Show your shoe.

Teddy bear, teddy bear,
That will do.

Teddy bear, teddy bear,
Run upstairs.

Teddy bear, teddy bear,
Say your prayers.

Teddy bear, teddy bear,
Turn out the light.

Teddy bear, teddy bear,
Say good night.

Little Jack Horner

Little Jack Horner
Sat in a corner,
Eating his Christmas pie.
He stuck in his thumb
And pulled out a plum
And said, "What a
     good boy am I!"

One, Two, Buckle My Shoe

One, two,
Buckle my shoe.

Three, four,
Shut the door.

Five, six,
Pick up sticks.

Seven, eight,
Lay them straight.

Nine, ten,
A good
fat hen.

Three Little Kittens

Three little kittens
Lost their mittens,
And they began to cry,
"Oh, mother, dear,
We sadly fear
Our mittens we have lost."

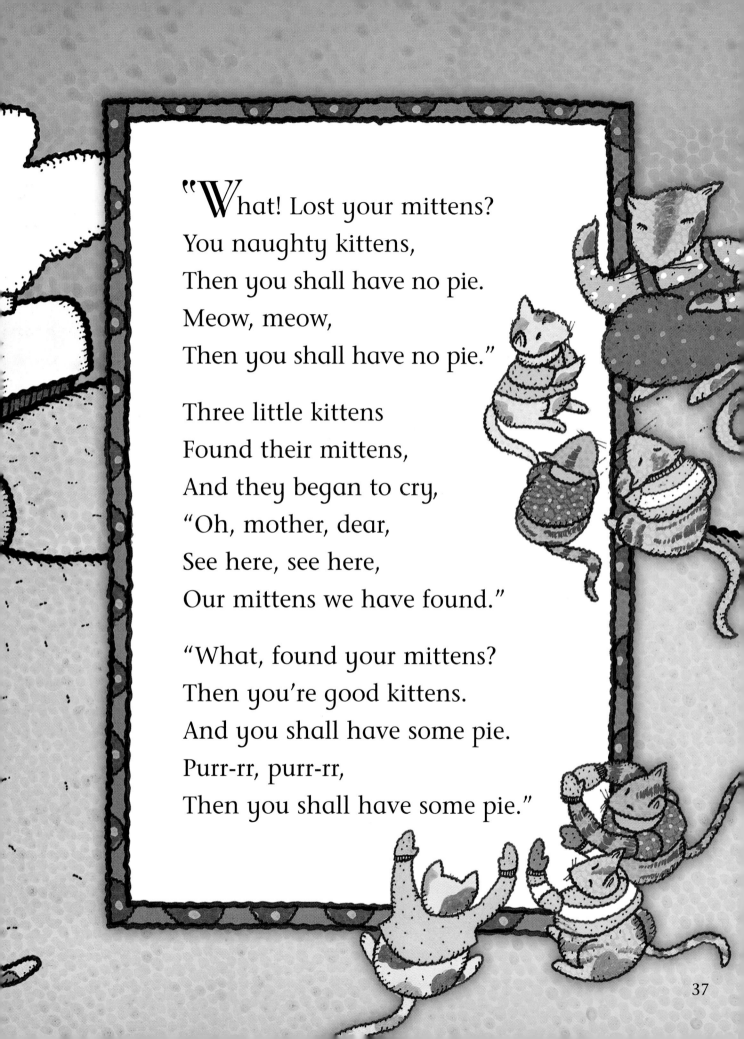

"What! Lost your mittens?
You naughty kittens,
Then you shall have no pie.
Meow, meow,
Then you shall have no pie."

Three little kittens
Found their mittens,
And they began to cry,
"Oh, mother, dear,
See here, see here,
Our mittens we have found."

"What, found your mittens?
Then you're good kittens.
And you shall have some pie.
Purr-rr, purr-rr,
Then you shall have some pie."

Mary, Mary, Quite Contrary

Mary, Mary, quite contrary,
How does your garden grow?
With silver bells and cockleshells
And pretty maids all in a row.

Bibliography
"Mother Goose Rhymes"

Edens, Cooper, ed. *The Glorious Mother Goose*. New York: Atheneum, 1998.
Illustrators include L. Leslie Brooke, Randolph Caldecott, Kate Greenaway,
Arthur Rackham, and others. This book of Mother Goose Rhymes is
beautifully illustrated with the work of classic children's book illustrators.

Engle, Kin. *Humpty Dumpty*. Dallas: Whispering Coyote Press, 1999.
This humorous, wonderfully illustrated narration of the great fall of the
world's most famous egg will delight children and parents alike.

Sechi-Johnson, Patricia. *Hickory, Dickory, Dock*. New York: Sterling, 1999.
This classic representation includes a finger puppet of the mouse to help
children recite the rhyme.

Buell Hale, Sarah Josepha. *Mary Had a Little Lamb*. New York: Orchard, 1995.
Salley Mavor uses appliqué, beads, and found objects to create unique
illustrations of Mary, her little lamb, and all the children in the classroom.

Galdone, Paul. *Three Little Kittens*. New York: Houghton Mifflin, 1988.
This delightful classic rhyme is beautifully illustrated by Paul Galdone. Yes,
those three little kittens finally find their mittens!

About "Goldilocks and the Three Bears"

"Goldilocks and the Three Bears," originally called "Tale of the Three Bears," first appeared in print in 1837, when Robert Southey included it in a collection of essays called *The Doctor*. Robert Southey was the poet laureate of England from 1813 to 1843. He was also considered a leading authority on Portuguese and Spanish history. Although he wrote many poems, biographies, tales, historical books, and articles, little of his work is known today. Scholars may be familiar with some of his epic poems and his *Life of Nelson* (1813), but he is best remembered for the "Tale of the Three Bears."

In Southey's original story, it was an old woman, not a little girl named Goldilocks, who intrudes on the bears. It wasn't until the publication of a book called *Aunt Friendly's Nursery Book*, in 1868, that the trespasser became a little girl with golden hair.

Retold by Roxanna Marino Knapp

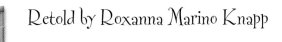

Goldilocks and the Three Bears

Illustrated by Laura J. Bryant

Once upon a time, there were three bears. They were Papa Bear, Mama Bear, and Baby Bear.

43

They each had a bowl to eat from. Papa Bear had a great big bowl.

Mama Bear had a medium bowl. Baby Bear had a tiny bowl.

They each had a chair to sit in. Papa Bear had a great big chair. Mama Bear had a medium chair. Baby Bear had a tiny chair.

They each had a bed to sleep in. Papa Bear had a great big bed. Mama Bear had a medium bed. Baby Bear had a tiny bed.

One morning, the bears made porridge.
The porridge was too hot, so they went
for a walk in the woods.

At about the same time, a girl named
Goldilocks was picking flowers nearby.
When she came to the house of the Three
Bears, Goldilocks knocked at the door.
Nobody answered.

Goldilocks smelled the porridge. It smelled so good that she went inside.

Goldilocks tasted the porridge in the great big bowl.
It was too hot.

Goldilocks tasted the porridge in the medium bowl. It was too cold.

Goldilocks tasted the porridge in the tiny bowl.
It was just right, so she ate it!

Then, Goldilocks needed to rest. She saw three chairs in the next room.

Goldilocks sat in the great big chair. It was too hard.

Goldilocks sat in the medium chair. It was too soft.

Goldilocks sat in the tiny chair. It was just right, but . . . oh, no! The chair broke apart!

Goldilocks still needed to rest. She was very tired.

She tried the great big bed. It was too hard.

She tried the medium bed. It was too soft.

She tried the tiny bed. It was just right, so she fell asleep.

Then the Three Bears came home. "Somebody has been eating my porridge!" boomed Papa Bear.

"Somebody has been eating my porridge!" cried Mama Bear.

"Somebody has been eating my porridge . . . and it's all gone!" squeaked Baby Bear.

"Somebody has been sitting in my chair!" boomed Papa Bear.

"Somebody has been sitting in my chair!" cried Mama Bear.

"Somebody has been sitting in my chair . . . and they broke it!" squeaked Baby Bear.

"Somebody has been sleeping in my bed!" boomed Papa Bear.

"Somebody has been sleeping in my bed!" cried Mama Bear.

"Somebody has been sleeping in my bed," squeaked Baby Bear, "and here she is!"

Goldilocks woke up at once. When she saw the Three Bears, she screamed.

Goldilocks jumped up and ran into the woods. The Three Bears never saw her again.

Bibliography
"Goldilocks and the Three Bears"

Brett, Jan. *Goldilocks and the Three Bears*. New York: Dodd Mead, 1992. This is a traditional retelling of the story of the little girl who invites herself into the house of the three bears, eats their food, sits on their chairs, and tries out their beds.

Campbell Ernst, Lisa. *Goldilocks Returns*. New York: Simon and Schuster, 2000. Goldilocks returns fifty years later to the bears' house to make amends for all the trouble she caused. This time, Goldilocks has a plan to set things right.

Freeman, Don. *Corduroy*. New York: Puffin, 1996. This charming story tells about the adventures of a teddy bear named Corduroy, who gets lost in a department store. He does find his way back to the toy department in time for a little girl to buy him and take him home.

Martin, Bill, Jr. *Brown Bear, Brown Bear, What Do You See?* New York: Henry Holt, 1996. Each page, beautifully illustrated by Eric Carle, introduces us to a new animal who uses rhythmic repetition to tell us which creature we will see next.

McPhail, David. *Lost!* Boston: Little Brown, 1990. A little boy meets a bear who is lost in the city. After the boy helps the bear find his way home, the boy realizes that he is now lost in the forest. The bear, who has become the boy's friend during the journey, returns the favor, setting out for the city again.

About "The Gingerbread Man"

The story of "The Gingerbread Man" or "The Gingerbread Boy" has been around since at least the nineteenth century. During that time, many versions of this folk tale were told in English-speaking countries. In 1890, Joseph Jacobs first recorded the story as "Johnny Cake" in his collection titled *English Fairy Stories*. But Jacobs found other versions, including an Irish story called "The Wonderful Cake" and a Scottish story called "The Wee Bunnock." He also found similarities with "The Fate of Mr. Jack Sparrow" in *Uncle Remus: His Songs and His Sayings*, Joel Chandler Harris's retellings of African-American tales.

Joseph Jacobs was born in Sydney, Australia, in 1854 and moved to England in 1872. There he became a respected folk tale scholar and a popular teller of fairy tales. He published collections of folk tales from England, Ireland, Italy, France, and India. In 1900, he moved to the United States, where he lived for the rest of his life working as revising editor on the *Jewish Encyclopedia*, teaching literature, and editing the magazine *American Hebrew*.

Retold by Roxanna Marino Knapp

The Gingerbread Man

Illustrated by Doug Bowles

Once, there was a lonely old couple. They wanted to have a child.

The old woman had an idea.
She would bake a gingerbread man.

The old woman mixed everything together.
She rolled out the dough and cut out a
gingerbread man. Then, she put him into
the oven to bake.

Later, the oven door popped open.
Out jumped the Gingerbread Man. The
woman cried, "Stop, Gingerbread Man!"
And she ran after him.

But the Gingerbread Man said,
"Run, run,
As fast as you can!
You can't catch me!
I'm the Gingerbread Man!"
And he ran and ran.

First, the Gingerbread Man met a cat.

The cat said, "Stop, Gingerbread Man!
I would like to eat you!"

But the Gingerbread Man said,
"Run, run,
As fast as you can!
You can't catch me!
I'm the Gingerbread Man!"

And he ran and ran.

Next, the Gingerbread Man
met a snake.

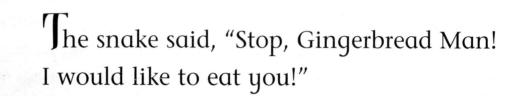

The snake said, "Stop, Gingerbread Man!
I would like to eat you!"

But the Gingerbread Man said,
"Run, run,
As fast as you can!
You can't catch me!
I'm the Gingerbread Man!"

And he ran and ran.

Then, the Gingerbread Man met a goose.

The goose said,
"Stop, Gingerbread Man!
I would like to eat you!"

But the Gingerbread Man said,
"Run, run,
As fast as you can!
You can't catch me!
I'm the Gingerbread Man!"

And he ran and ran.

Then, the Gingerbread Man met a fox.

By now, the Gingerbread Man felt very proud
of himself.

He had run away from a little old woman. He had
run away from a little old man.

He had run away from a cat. He had
run away from a snake. And he
had run away from a goose.

So the Gingerbread Man said,
"Run, run,
As fast as you can!
You can't catch me!
I'm the Gingerbread Man!"

"Why, I wouldn't think of catching you!" said the sly fox.

"But there is a river ahead," said the fox. "I can help you cross it."

"Yes! Yes!" cried the Gingerbread Man. "I can't get wet!"

"Jump onto my tail," said the fox.

"Look, the river is deep," said the fox.
"Jump onto my back!"

"Now, the river is very deep," said the fox. "Jump onto my nose!"

Then, the fox opened
its mouth . . .

. . . and that was the end of the Gingerbread Man!

Bibliography
"The Gingerbread Man"

Galdone, Paul. *The Gingerbread Boy*. New York: Clarion, 1975. This is a classic retelling of the tale of the Gingerbread Boy who is able to run away from everyone . . . everyone except a certain sly fox, that is.

Amoss, Berthe. *The Cajun Gingerbread Boy*. New York: Hyperion, 1994. In this Cajun version of the tale, it is M'sieur Cocodrie, the alligator, who is the Gingerbread Boy's ruination.

Morris, Ann. *Bread, Bread, Bread*. New York: Lothrop, Lee & Shepard, 1989. Did the story of the Gingerbread Man make you hungry? Then you will be ravenous after reading Ann Morris's simple text and feasting your eyes on Ken Heyman's beautiful photographs of different types of bread enjoyed around the world.

Carle, Eric. *Pancakes, Pancakes!* Saxonville, MA: Picture Book Studio, 1990. Jack wakes up with a craving for a big pancake. Jack must first work hard to gather all the ingredients. No supermarket mix for him. He begins with cutting the wheat!

Numeroff, Laura Joffe. *If You Give a Moose a Muffin*. New York: HarperCollins, 1991. This delightful story follows a young boy and his uninvited visitor—a moose—through a series of silly antics.

About "Little Red Riding Hood"

The first version of "Little Red Riding Hood" known to have been recorded was told by Charles Perrault, a French poet and storyteller. He was a serious scholar of literature, but the tales included in his *Contes de ma mère l'oye (Tales of Mother Goose)*, published in 1697, are most appealing for their charming simplicity. The collection included other classic stories such as "The Sleeping Beauty" and "Puss in Books."

Another well-known version of "Little Red Riding Hood" is the German tale "Little Red Cap" from the Brothers Grimm. Jacob and Wilhelm Grimm traveled through German villages during the early nineteenth century, collecting and publishing tales that were traditionally told orally. They also gathered material from printed sources and tales from Scandinavia, Finland, Spain, the Netherlands, Great Britain, and Serbia. In 1812, they published the first volume of *Kinder und Hausmärchen (Children's and Household Tales)*. The brothers would eventually publish two hundred fairy tales, ten children's legends, some six hundred sagas, and six hundred folk songs, as well as scholarly works on literature and linguistics.

Other versions of "Little Red Riding Hood" have been told around the world. One of these is a Chinese version called "Lon Po Po," in which three little girls outsmart a terrifying wolf.

Retold by Roxanna Marino Knapp

Little Red Riding Hood

Illustrated by Tammie Lyon

Once upon a time, there was a little girl. The little girl's grandmother loved her very much. The little girl's grandmother wanted to give her something special. So she made the girl a cape.

The cape had a
wonderful hood.
And it was the girl's
favorite color—red.

The little girl wore her cape everywhere! She wore it to the store.

She wore it to visit friends.

She even wore it to bed!
People started calling her
Little Red Riding Hood.

One day, Little Red Riding Hood's mother said, "Grandmother is sick. Please take this basket of food to her." Then, her mother said, "Remember, do not go off the path. Hurry along now!"

Little Red Riding Hood began her long walk. On her way through the woods, she met a wolf.

"Good morning," said the wolf.

"Good morning," said Little Red Riding Hood.

"Where are you going so early?" asked the wolf.

"To Grandmother's house," she said.

"Where does she live?" asked the wolf.

"On top of that hill," said Little Red Riding Hood.

"Hmmm," thought the wolf. "I can run to Grandmother's house! I can get there first! Then, I'll have my own picnic lunch!" he thought. "I'll eat them both!"

"Well, good-bye, Little Red Riding Hood!" said the wolf. And off he ran towards Grandmother's house.

Once there, the wolf sneaked inside.

Then, he sneaked into Grandmother's bedroom.

Suddenly, Grandmother woke up. "Oh!" she cried.

"Quiet!" hissed the wolf. He opened the closet door. "I'll put you in here for now. And I'll eat you later."

The wolf found another nightshirt and nightcap. He would pretend to be Little Red Riding Hood's grandmother.

Just then, Little Red Riding Hood arrived. She knocked on the door.

"Come in, dear," said the wolf in a high voice. Little Red Riding Hood walked into the room.

"Grandmother, what big ears you have!" said Little Red Riding Hood.

"The better to hear you with!" said the wolf.

"Grandmother, what big eyes you
have!" said Little Red Riding Hood.

"The better to see you with!"
said the wolf.

"Grandmother, what big hands you have!" said Little Red Riding Hood.

"The better to hold you with!" said the wolf.

"Grandmother, what BIG teeth you have!" said Little Red Riding Hood.

"The better to EAT you with!" shouted the wolf.

And he leaped toward Little Red Riding Hood. But she jumped out of the way so fast . . .

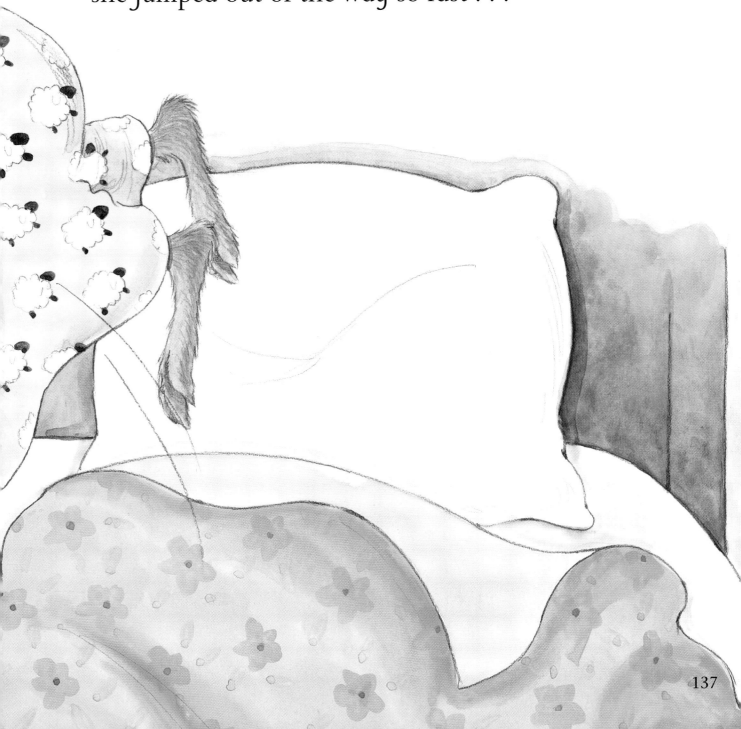

. . . that the wolf sailed right out the window. He rolled down the hill and just kept going!

Little Red Riding Hood helped Grandmother out of the closet. "The wolf is gone now," she said.

"Good!" said Grandmother.

Then, Grandmother and Little
Red Riding Hood shared their
picnic lunch.

Bibliography
"Little Red Riding Hood"

Grimm, Jacob and Wilhelm. *Little Red Riding Hood*. New York: Holiday, 1986. This classic retelling is illustrated by Trina Schart Hyman. Grandmother and Red Riding Hood are eaten alive by the wolf and then saved by a kind woodsman, but there is no graphic violence in the richly detailed pictures.

Ernst, Lisa Campbell. *Little Red Riding Hood: A Newfangled Prairie Tale*. New York: Simon & Schuster, 1995. This modern Red Riding Hood encounters the wolf while delivering muffins to her not-so-frail granny out working on the Midwestern prairie. This wolf is out to get Granny's secret muffin recipe, which is included for readers.

Young, Ed. *Lon Po Po: A Red-Riding Hood Story from China*. New York: Philomel, 1989. In this ancient Chinese story, three sisters left at home while their mother goes to visit their sick grandmother outwit a wolf disguised as the grandmother. This book, translated and illustrated by Ed Young, was the 1990 winner of the Caldecott Medal, awarded to the illustrator of the year's most distinguished American picture book for children.

dePaola, Tomie. *Nana Upstairs, Nana Downstairs*. New York: G. P. Putnam's Sons, 1998. This story gently handles the concept of death as it tells of a little boy's relationships with his grandmother and great-grandmother.

Patrick, Denise Lewis. *Red Dancing Shoes*. New York: Tambourine, 1993. This book is illustrated with paintings by James E. Ransome. A little girl gets a special gift from her grandmother—a pair of red dancing shoes. She feels magical as she dances in them, until she goes to visit her aunt and falls into the mud.

About "The Three Little Pigs"

"The Three Little Pigs" was a folk tale that J. O. Halliwell recorded in 1853 as he was making a collection of such tales. It was printed in 1890 in *English Fairy Tales* and edited by the folklore scholar Joseph Jacobs.

Interestingly enough, Joseph Jacobs believed that the pigs were originally kids, or baby goats. This idea was based on the line with which the pigs answer the wolf: "Not by the hair on my chinny, chin, chin." Pigs do not have much hair on their chins, but kids do. Also, "The Three Little Pigs" is very similar to a story recorded by the Brothers Grimm called "The Wolf and the Seven Little Kids." Fortunately, readers never believed that the story was about kids, so "The Three Little Pigs" remains the classic pig story we know today.

Joseph Jacobs, born in Sydney, Australia, in 1854, moved to England in 1872. There he became a respected folk tale scholar and a popular teller of fairy tales. He published collections of folk tales from England, Ireland, Italy, France, and India. In 1900, he moved to the United States, where he lived for the rest of his life. There he worked as revising editor on the Jewish Encyclopedia, taught literature, and edited the magazine American Hebrew.

Retold by Roxanna Marino Knapp

The Three Little Pigs

Illustrated by Horacio Elena

Once upon a time, there were three little pigs. One day, they left home to make their way in the world.

All summer long, the pigs had fun.
They made lots of friends.

But soon, fall arrived. Everyone began getting ready for winter. It started to rain. Then, the wind started to blow.

The pigs needed to build homes.

The first pig thought for a moment. "I'll build my house from straw," he said.

*H*e was sure that it would take less than a day.

The other two pigs were not happy with the straw house. "It's not strong enough!" they said.

The second pig thought for a moment.
"I'll build my house from sticks," he said.

*H*e was sure it would take only a day.

The third pig was not happy with the stick house.
"It's not strong enough!" he said.

The third pig thought for a moment. "I'll build my house from brick," he said.

*H*e knew it would take a whole week. But, he knew it would be a strong house.

The other two pigs were not happy with the brick house. "It took too long!" they said.

The third pig spotted some wolf tracks. All three pigs rushed to their homes for safety.

First, the wolf came to the house made of straw. "Little pig, little pig, let me come in!" said the wolf.

"Not by the hair on my chinny, chin, chin!" cried the first little pig.

"Then, I'll huff, and I'll puff, and I'll blow your house down!" yelled the wolf.

And that is just what he did. The wolf blew down the house made of straw.

Next, the wolf came to the house made of sticks. "Little pigs, little pigs, let me come in!" said the wolf.

"Not by the hair on our chinny, chin, chins!" cried the pigs.

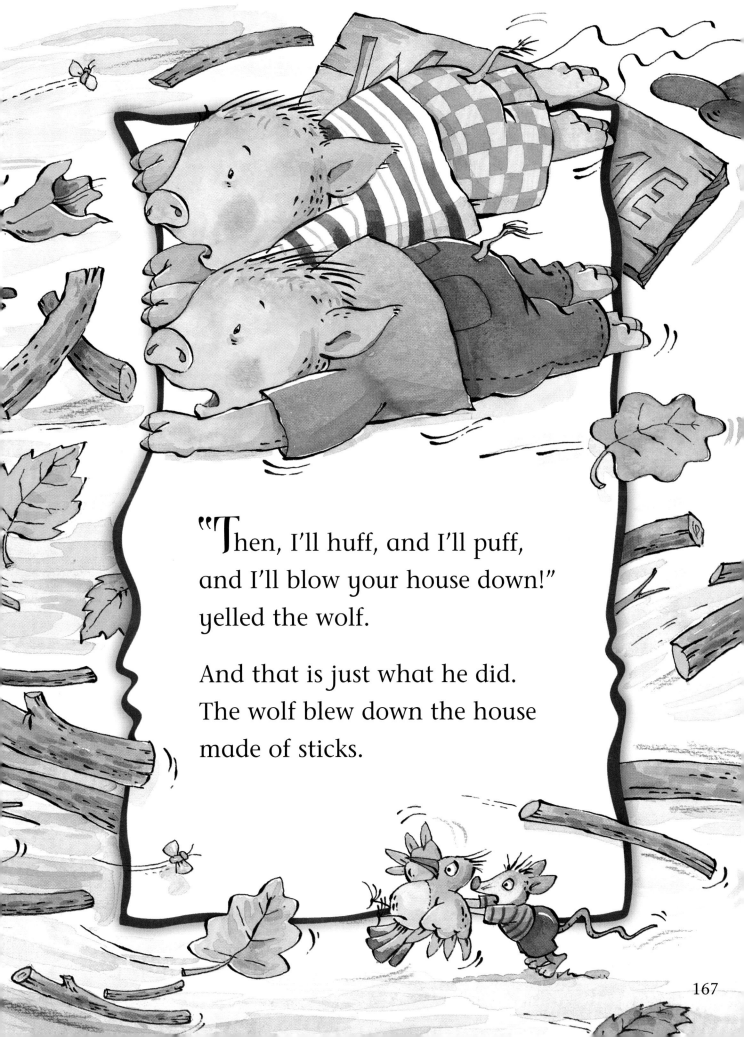

"Then, I'll huff, and I'll puff, and I'll blow your house down!" yelled the wolf.

And that is just what he did. The wolf blew down the house made of sticks.

Then, the wolf came to the house made of bricks. "Little pigs, little pigs, let me come in!" said the wolf.

"Not by the hair on our chinny, chin, chins!" cried the pigs.

"Then, I'll huff, and I'll puff, and I'll blow your house down!" yelled the wolf.

The wolf huffed and he puffed . . . but nothing happened. He puffed and he huffed . . . but still nothing happened.

The wolf was not about to give up. He ran toward the chimney.

The third pig guessed what the wolf was doing. He quickly lit a fire in the fireplace.

The wolf started down the chimney. Then, his tail began to burn!

The wolf scrambled out of the chimney and started to run. He kept on running and was never seen again!

Bibliography
"The Three Little Pigs"

Galdone, Paul. *The Three Little Pigs*. New York: Houghton Mifflin, 1979. This is one of Paul Galdone's many folk tale retellings. In classic language and charming illustration, he faithfully retells the story of those famous little pigs.

Kellogg, Steven. *The Three Little Pigs*. New York: Morrow, 1997. In this updated version, three piglets—Percy, Pete, and Prudence—refuse to let a hungry wolf named Tempesto make breakfast out of them.

McPhail, David. *Pigs Aplenty, Pigs Galore!* New York: Dutton, 1993. In this humorous and cleverly rhymed story, the narrator relates what happens when pigs, more pigs, and even more pigs invade his home.

Newton-John, Olivia. *A Pig Tale*. New York: Simon & Schuster, 1993. Ziggy the pig is very embarrassed by all the junk his father, Iggy, collects, until he understands that his pop is using all the junk to make a special invention. This is a delightful story about reusing items and saving the earth!

Morris, Ann. *Houses and Homes*. New York: Lothrop, Lee & Shepard, 1992. Through Ken Heyman's beautiful photographs, we are able to travel throughout the world to see homes of different cultures and regions—yes, even some made partly of straw!

About "The Three Billy Goats Gruff"

"The Three Billy Goats Gruff" is one of the many Norwegian folk tales collected and published by Peter Asbjørnsen and Jørgen Moe. These Norwegian men met each other in 1827, when they were teenagers. They became very close friends but soon moved apart to complete their education. At the age of twenty, Asbjørnsen became a tutor in eastern Norway and began to collect folk tales. Moe graduated and also became a tutor. Not knowing of Asbjørnsen's hobby, he also began to collect folk tales during his vacations in the southern part of Norway. When they discovered their common interest, Asbjørnsen and Moe decided to combine their efforts and publish their works together. Their collections of folk tales became so popular that their names are hardly ever seen separately, but always as Asbjørnsen and Moe.

Asbjørnsen and Moe were successful because they used simple language in their retellings. They were also careful to keep the Norwegian traditions of storytelling, such as this ending of "The Three Billy Goats Gruff":

And so snip, snap, snout!
Now my tale's told out.

Soon after Asbjørnsen and Moe's collection was published, Jacob Grimm suggested to the Englishman Sir George Dasent that he translate the tales into English. "The Three Billy Goats Gruff" was one of the tales that appeared in 1859 in Dasent's collection *Popular Tales from the Norse.*

Retold by Roxanna Marino Knapp

The Three Billy Goats Gruff

Illustrated by Ilene Richards

nce upon a time, there were three billy goats. Their name was Gruff.

The three Billy Goats Gruff loved to eat green grass. Day in and day out, they ate sweet, green grass!

One day, all the sweet, green grass was gone. The three Billy Goats Gruff were very hungry.

They remembered that more grass grew near the river. So, off went the three Billy Goats Gruff.

The three Billy Goats Gruff arrived at the river. On the other side was the greenest grass they had ever seen.

But under the bridge lived a big, nasty troll. The troll had eyes as big as saucers. He had a nose as long as a poker.

What were the goats to do?
They got together and came up
with a plan.

The smallest Billy Goat Gruff went across the
bridge first.

"TRIP, TRAP, TRIP, TRAP!" went the first goat's little feet on the bridge.

"Who's that trip-trapping on my bridge?" roared the troll.

The first goat had a tiny voice. "It is I, the smallest Billy Goat Gruff," he said in his tiny voice.

"I'm going to get you!" said the troll.

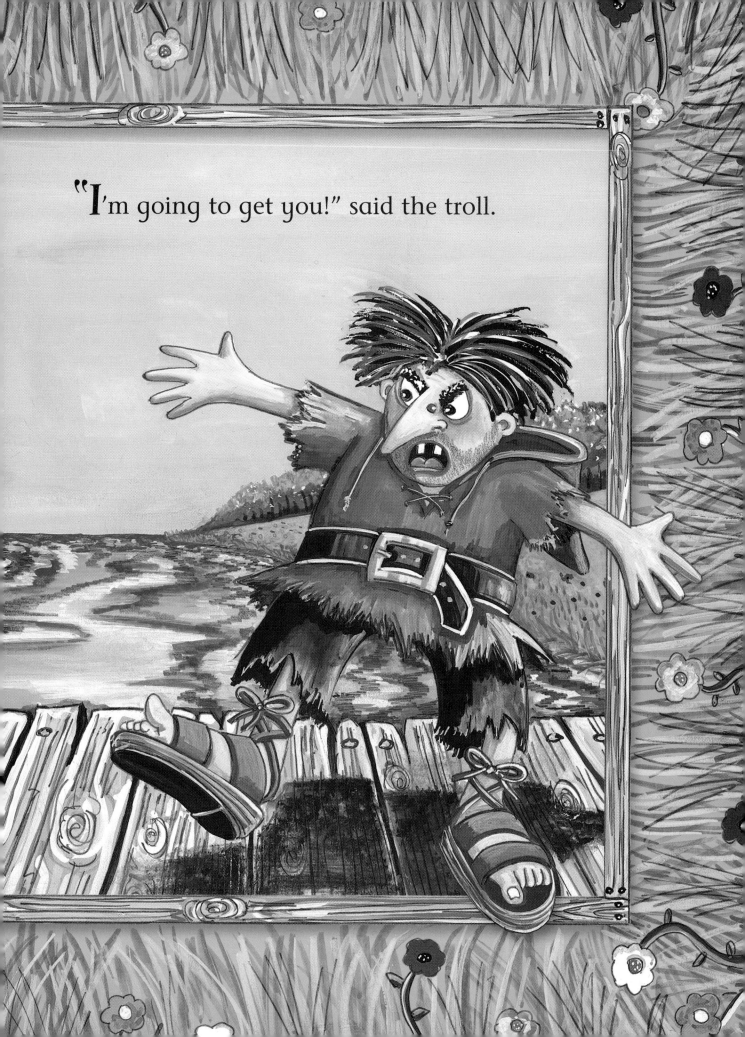

"Oh, no!" said the smallest Billy Goat Gruff. "I'm too little! Wait for my brother. He is much bigger."

The troll said, "Then be on your way!"

The second Billy Goat Gruff came to the bridge. "TRIP, TRAP, TRIP, TRAP!" went the second goat's not-so-little feet on the bridge.

"Who's that trip-trapping on my bridge?" roared the troll.

The second goat had a bigger voice. "It is I, the second Billy Goat Gruff," he said in his bigger voice.

"I'm going to get you!" said the troll.

"Oh, no!" said the second Billy Goat Gruff. "I'm too little! Wait for my brother. He is much bigger."

The troll said, "Then be on your way!"

Just then, the biggest Billy Goat Gruff came along. "TRIP, TRAP, TRIP, TRAP!" went the biggest goat's heavy feet on the bridge.

"Who's that trip-trapping on my bridge?" roared the troll.

The third goat had a great big voice.
"IT IS I, THE BIGGEST BILLY GOAT
GRUFF!" he said.

"I'm going to get you!" said the troll.

"No, you won't!" said the goat. "I will get you with my great big horns!"

The troll ran at the biggest Billy Goat Gruff. But the billy goat knocked the troll right off the bridge.

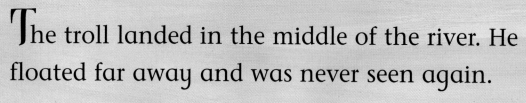

The troll landed in the middle of the river. He floated far away and was never seen again.

The three Billy Goats Gruff were happy to be across the river.

There, they could eat all the sweet, green grass they wanted.

Some say they are still there today. And so, snip, snap, snout! This tale is told out!

Bibliography
"The Three Billy Goats Gruff"

Stevens, Janet. *The Three Billy Goats Gruff*. San Diego: Harcourt Brace, 1995. This story is true to the traditional tale of the three brothers Gruff who outwit a troll to get across a bridge.

Granowsky, Alvin. *The Three Billy Goats Gruff/Just a Friendly Old Troll (Another Point of View)*. Austin: Raintree/Steck-Vaughn, 1996. Once children have read the original tale, they will probably thoroughly enjoy hearing the story from the point of view of the misunderstood troll.

Grimm, Jacob and Wilhelm. *The Wolf and the Seven Little Kids*. New York: North South: 1995. A wolf eats six of seven little kids (goats) alive, and while he is sleeping, the mother goat rescues them. The illustrations by Bernadette Watts are humorous and not graphic. This story also lends itself to comparison with "Little Red Riding Hood."

Sharmat, Mitchell. *Gregory, the Terrible Eater*. New York: Simon & Schuster, 1980. In this story, illustrated by José Aruego and Ariane Dewey, a goat named Gregory is a very picky eater, not like the other goats who are happily eating shoes and tin cans. The nonconformist Gregory prefers to eat fruits and vegetables instead.

Kimmel, Eric A. *Boots and His Brothers: A Norwegian Tale*. New York: Holiday House: 1992. For another sample of a Norwegian folk tale, share this story of a young man who receives a magic ax and a magic shovel as his reward for his kindness to an old beggar woman.

Reading Activities

A Tall Wall

Look! Humpty Dumpty is sitting on a tall wall. Let's hope he doesn't fall! Look at all of the pictures on the wall. Draw a line to connect the pictures with rhyming names.

Hand-y Rhymes

Mother
Goose
Rhymes

Make up your own hand motions or fingerplays to retell the Mother Goose rhymes. Here are two examples.

Little Miss Muffet

Little Miss Muffet
Sat on a tuffet (Make a fist and leave thumb standing.)
Eating her curds and whey.
　　(Pretend to "feed" thumb.)
Along came a spider, (Run fingers along arm.)
Who sat down beside her
　　(Stop fingers at fist with thumb.)
And frightened Miss Muffet away.
　　(Throw hands up in the air.)

Hickory, Dickory, Dock

Hickory, dickory, dock.
　　(Hold left arm above your head.)
The mouse ran up the clock.
　　(Run fingers of right hand up your left arm.)
The clock struck one. (Hold one index finger up.)
The mouse ran down! (Run fingers down arm.)
Hickory, dickory, dock. (Hold arm above your head.)

Comprehension/Retelling　　　　　Read and Learn With Classic Stories—Grade K

J Is for Jack and Jill

Jack and **Jill** both have names that begin with the sound of **j**. Look at the pictures. Write **j** on the line if the picture name begins with the sound of **j**.

Mother Goose Rhymes

Shoes for This and That

Do you remember the old woman who lived in a shoe? There are many different kinds of shoes. Draw a line to match each shoe with its activity.

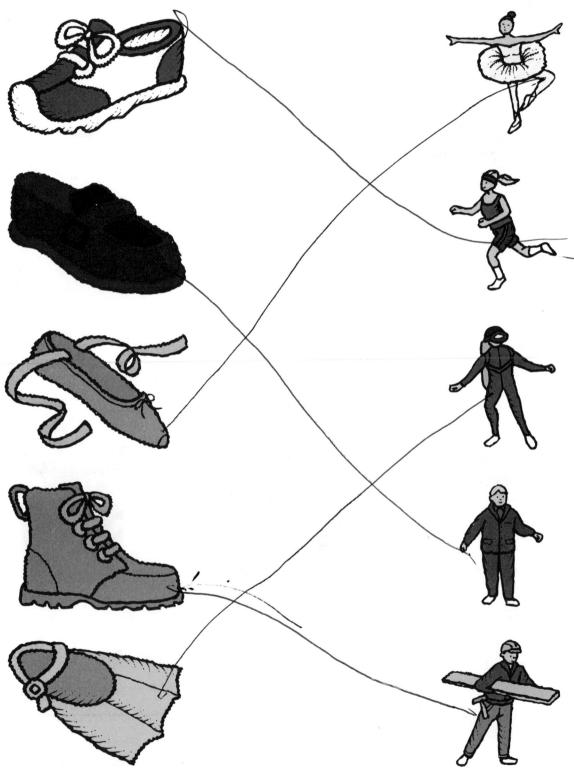

Shell for Short e

Shell has the sound of **short e**. Circle the things in the pumpkin shell that have the sound of **short e**.

Mother
Goose
Rhymes

Sky High

What do you see when you look up in the sky? Color each thing that you might see in the sky.

Comprehension/Categorizing

Read and Learn With Classic Stories—Grade K

What Color Is It?

Read the color words in the list. Then, color each animal the correct color.

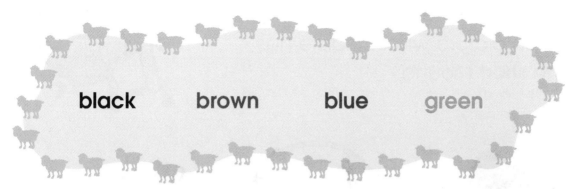

black   **brown**   **blue**   green

a green frog

a brown horse

a black sheep

a blue fish

Mother Goose Rhymes

The Dish Ran Away
With the Spoon

Dish has the sound of **short i**. Say the name of each picture. Circle each picture whose name has the **short i** sound.

Phonics/Short Vowel i   **Read and Learn With Classic Stories—Grade K**

Going Shopping

Here are some things you may find when you go the market, or grocery store. Draw a line to match the picture with its name.

apples

peanut butter

bread

jam

grapes

School Days

Mary's lamb can't really read a book in school! Look at the pictures. Put an **X** on the pictures that show something that could **not** really happen in school.

Comprehension/Reality and Fantasy   **Read and Learn With Classic Stories—Grade K**

Teddy Bear Time

It's time to finish the picture of the teddy bear. Follow the directions.

1. Draw a  on the teddy bear.

2. Color his blue.

3. Draw a on his face.

4. Color his red.

What Goes In It?

Draw lines from the pie to each thing that you could bake in a pie. Then, draw lines from the garden to each thing you could grow in a garden.

Comprehension/Draw Conclusions

Read and Learn With Classic Stories—Grade K

Number Match-Up

Say the rhyme "One, Two, Buckle My Shoe." As you say the words, circle the picture that goes with each set of numbers.

1, 2, . . .

3, 4, . . .

5, 6, . . .

7, 8, . . .

9, 10, . . .

Lost!

Help the kittens find their lost mittens! Connect the pictures whose names begin with the sound of **l**.

Mother
Goose
Rhymes

I'll Tell You a Story

Color the finger puppets. Then, cut them out and tape the bottoms together to make rings. Use the puppets to tell the story of "Goldilocks and the Three Bears."

Goldilocks and the Three Bears

What Happens Next?

Cut out the pictures below. Put them in the order they happened in the story. Then, glue the pictures in the correct order onto another sheet of paper.

Glue

How Do They Feel?

Look at the pictures below. Color the face that shows how each character feels.

Goldilocks and the Three Bears

Meet My Family

The family of the Three Bears includes Baby Bear, Mama Bear, and Papa Bear. Who is in your family? Draw your family in the box below. Show your family members in order from smallest to largest.

Goldilocks and the Three Bears

Comprehension/Classifying by Size

Read and Learn With Classic Stories—Grade K

Rhyme Time

Goldilocks and Baby Bear are playing a rhyming game together. Cut out the picture cards. Then, match the pictures whose names rhyme. Say the rhyming words.

B Is for Bear

Bear begins with the sound of **b**. Color the pictures whose names begin with the **b** sound.

Goldilocks and the Three Bears

What Does Not Belong?

Goldilocks does not belong with Baby Bear, Mama Bear, and Papa Bear. Look at the pictures below. Draw an **X** on the picture in each row that **does not** belong.

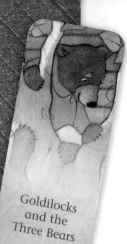

Goldilocks
and the
Three Bears

Comprehension/Classifying

Read and Learn With Classic Stories—Grade K

What's Cooking?

What will the Three Bears cook up next? Look at the ingredients in each box. Then, color the food you think the Three Bears will make.

 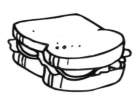 

Goldilocks and the Three Bears

G Is for Goldilocks

Goldilocks begins with the sound of **g**. Write **g** next to each picture whose name begins with the **g** sound.

Goldilocks and the Three Bears

Phonics/Consonant g

Read and Learn With Classic Stories—Grade K

Hot and Cold

Words like **hot** and **cold** are called **opposites**. Circle the two pictures in each row that show opposites.

Goldilocks and the Three Bears

Hello, Neighbor!

What do you think would happen if the Three Bears came to Goldilocks' house? Tell what you think would happen. Then, draw a picture to show it.

Comprehension/Predicting   Read and Learn With Classic Stories—Grade K

We Go Together

Look at the pictures in each row, and circle the two that go together. Then, tell why they go together.

The
Gingerbread
Man

My Favorite Part

What is your favorite part of the story? Draw a picture showing it. Tell someone else about your picture.

M Is for Man

Man begins with the sound of **m**. Color the space red if the name of the picture in it begins with the **m** sound. What letter do you see?

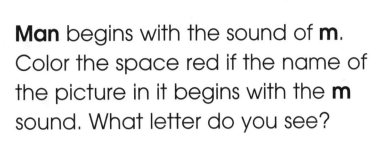

Listen for Short a

Cat has the **short a** sound. Print
a on the line if the picture
name has the **short a** sound.

_a_ _a_

_a_ _a_

_a_ _a_

Phonics/Short Vowel **a**

Read and Learn With Classic Stories—Grade K

Rhyme Time Game

Play this rhyming game with a friend.

How to play:

1. Cut out the cards. Mix them up and put them facedown.
2. Take turns turning over two cards. If they rhyme, keep them. If they do not, put them back.
3. Keep playing until all the cards have been used.

The Gingerbread Man

Could It Really Happen?

It's fun to make believe that a gingerbread man can run fast, isn't it? But a gingerbread man really can't run at all. Color the pictures that show things that could really happen.

The Gingerbread Man

Make a Gingerbread Man

Make your own Gingerbread Man. Ask an adult to help you.

Recipe for: _____ **Gingerbread Cookies** _____

Ingredients:

$\frac{1}{2}$	cup soft margarine
$\frac{3}{4}$	cup packed light brown sugar
2	eggs
$\frac{3}{4}$	cup light molasses
$4\frac{1}{2}$	cups all-purpose flour
2	teaspoons ground cinnamon
2	teaspoons ground ginger
$\frac{1}{2}$	teaspoon ground nutmeg
2	teaspoons baking soda
$\frac{1}{4}$	teaspoon salt

Directions:

1. Beat the margarine and sugar with an electric mixer.

2. Add the eggs and molasses. Mix them until they are smooth.

3. Mix the flour, baking soda, salt, and spices in another bowl.

4. Mix all the ingredients together and stir.

5. Divide the dough in half. Wrap it in wax paper, and chill it for several hours.

6. Roll out a small amount of dough onto a floured surface.

7. Use a cookie cutter to make your own gingerbread men.

8. Put them on a greased cookie sheet.

9. Bake at 350°F for 8 to 10 minutes.

10. Let the cookies cool. Then, decorate and enjoy your gingerbread men!

The Gingerbread Man

Gingerbread Cookies

Making gingerbread cookies sure is fun! Circle the picture in each row that shows something you use to make gingerbread cookies.

The Gingerbread Man

  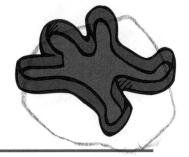

Listen for Short o

Fox has the **short o** sound. Color the pictures whose names have the **short o** sound.

The
Gingerbread
Man

As Fast As You Can!

In the story, the Gingerbread Man was **fast**. Put an **X** on the picture in each box that shows something that moves **fast**.

The Gingerbread Man

A New Ending

How else could the story of "The Gingerbread Man" have ended? Draw a new ending to the story. Tell about your new ending.

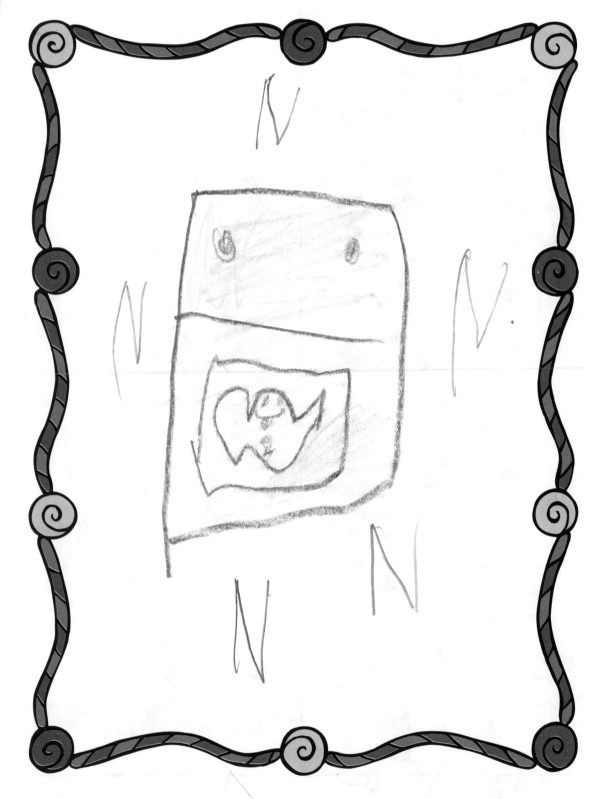

Comprehension/Predicting

Read and Learn With Classic Stories—Grade K

Real or Make-Believe?

Look at the pictures. Circle each picture that shows something real. Put an **X** on each picture that shows something make-believe.

Little
Red Riding
Hood

Which One Is Different?

Look at the pictures in each row. Circle the one that is different. Tell how it is different.

Little
Red Riding
Hood

256   Visual Discrimination/Same and Different   Read and Learn With Classic Stories—Grade K

It Begins With H

Hood begins with the sound of **h**. Help Little Red Riding Hood look for things that begin with the sound of **h**. Circle those things in the picture.

Little
Red Riding
Hood

Let's Have a Picnic!

Go on a picnic with Little Red Riding Hood. Which things will you need for your picnic? Draw a line from each thing you will need to the picnic blanket.

Comprehension/Classification

Read and Learn With Classic Stories—Grade K

W Is for Wolf

Wolf begins with the sound of **w**. Go shopping with the wolf. Color all of the things in the store that begin with the sound of **w**.

Little Red Riding Hood

A Picture of Grandmother

Finish this picture of Little Red Riding Hood's grandmother. Give her **eyes**, **ears**, **hands**, and **teeth**. Talk about what each body part is used for. Then, draw a line from the word to the body part.

eyes

ears

teeth

hands

Match Up (page 2)

Little Red Riding Hood

basket

house

glasses

Going to Grandma's House

Little Red Riding Hood is going to Grandmother's house. Which is the shorter path? Color that path **blue**. Color the longer path **orange**. Color the trees **green** and **brown**. Color the flowers **red**.

Little Red Riding Hood

A Special Time

Little
Red Riding
Hood

Draw a picture about a special time you had with a grandparent or other family member. Show your drawing and tell about it. Then, write some words or a sentence about it.

Writing/Description

Read and Learn With Classic Stories—Grade K

Act It Out

Color and cut out the puppets below. Tape a craft stick, a straw, or a pencil to the back of each puppet. Then, cut out the houses on page 269. Use the puppets and the houses to tell the story of "The Three Little Pigs."

The Three Little Pigs

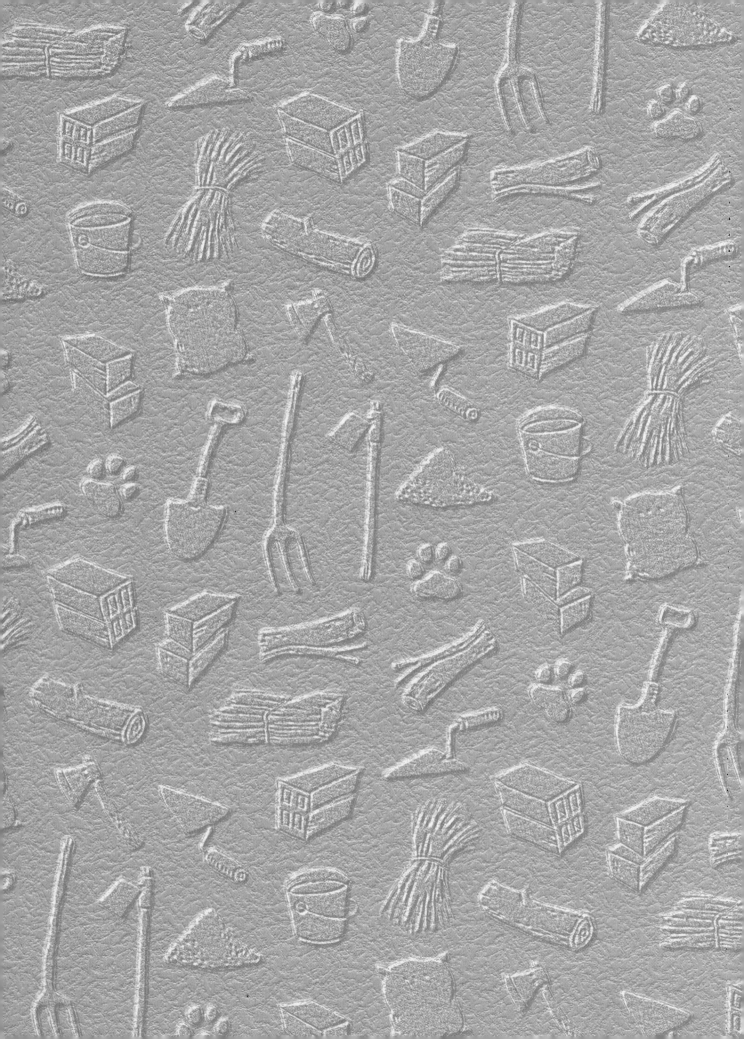

Act It Out (page 2)

The
Three Little
Pigs

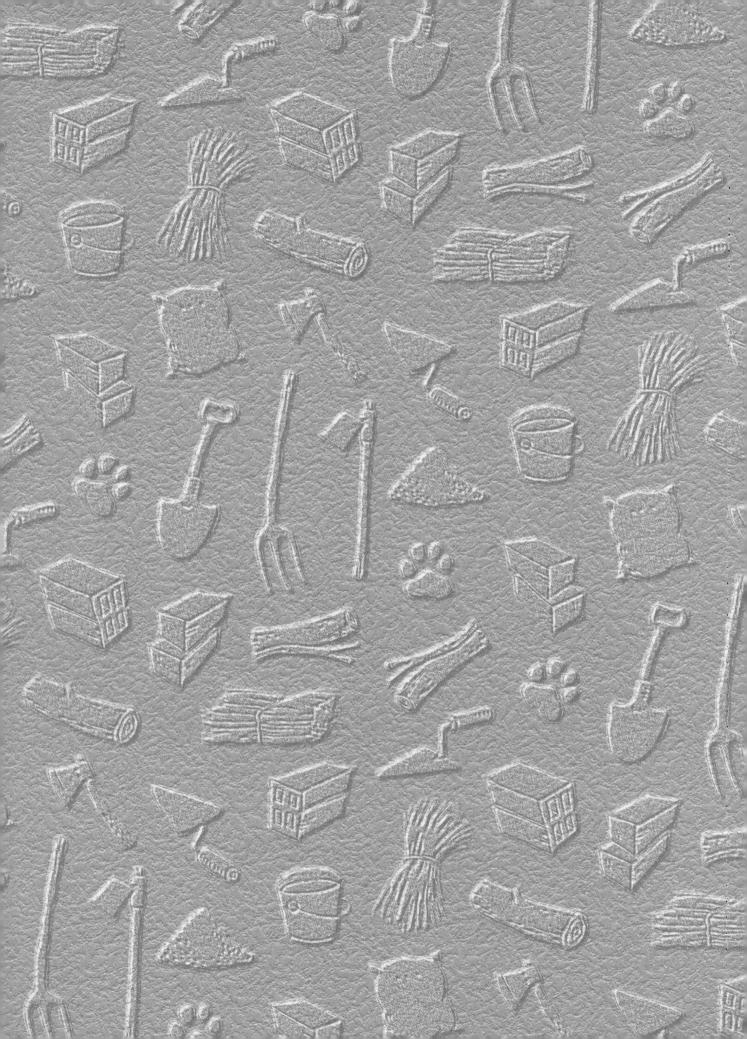

One, Two, Three

Words can stand for numbers. Look at each picture, and write the correct number word on the line.

one　　　　**two**　　　　**three**

The Three Little Pigs

one

two

three

two

one

three

Home, Sweet Home

The Three Little Pigs made their homes from different things. Circle the homes that were built with the same things that the pigs used.

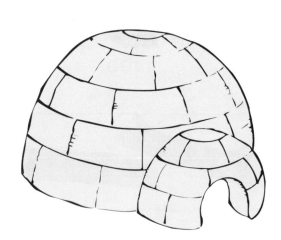

Comprehension/Same and Different

Read and Learn With Classic Stories—Grade K

Two of a Kind

Look at the pictures in each row. Circle the two pictures that are alike in some way. Then, tell why they are alike.

The Three Little Pigs

It's a Party!

The Three Little Pigs are so glad the wolf is gone that they are going to have a big party. Look at the party items in each box. Put an **X** on the item that is different in some way. Then, tell how it is different.

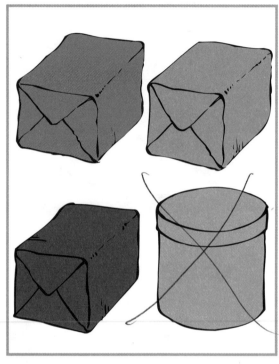

Visual Discrimination/Same and Different

Read and Learn With Classic Stories—Grade K

Tell the Order

Think about the story. Write the numbers 1, 2, 3, and 4 in the boxes to show the correct order.

The Three Little Pigs

Which One Doesn't Belong?

The wolf does not belong with the Three Little Pigs. Draw an **X** on the picture that **does not** belong in each row. Then, tell why it doesn't belong.

Comprehension/Classifying

Read and Learn With Classic Stories—Grade K

What Rhymes With Pig?

Look at the pictures. Which ones rhyme with pig?
Trace the words that rhyme with pig.

cat   wig   dig

hat   sit   twig

Pig Begins With P

Pig begins with the sound of **p**.
Look at the picture of the Three
Little Pigs' picnic in the park.
Color all the things that begin
with the sound of **p**.

Phonics/Consonant p

Read and Learn With Classic Stories—Grade K

Pig Ends With G

Pig begins with **p** but it ends with **g**. Say the name of each picture. Listen for the ending sound. Color the pictures whose names end with the sound of **g**.

The Three Little Pigs

And Then . . .

Draw a picture about what you think the Three Little Pigs did after the wolf ran away. Tell about your picture.

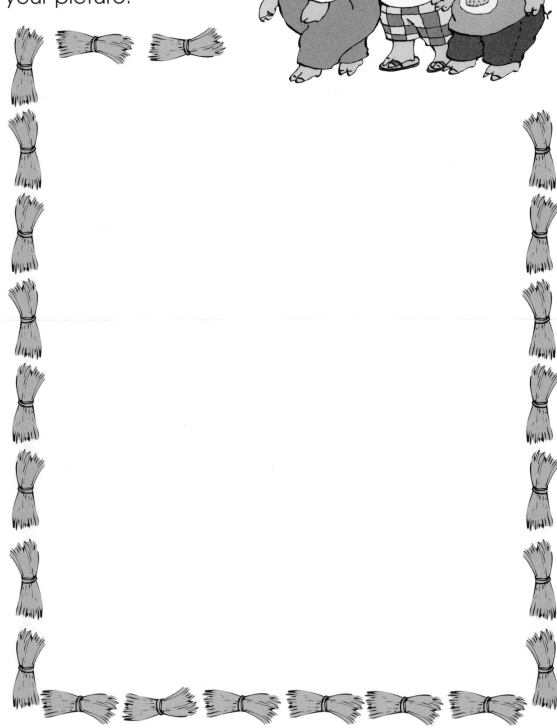

Comprehension/Predicting

Read and Learn With Classic Stories—Grade K

Tell It Like It Is

Cut out the characters on this page. Then, glue each character to a craft stick or an old sock to make a puppet. Now, use the characters to tell the story of "The Three Billy Goats Gruff."

The Three Billy Goats Gruff

First, Second, Third

The words **first**, **second**, and **third** tell about order. Follow the directions.

first   second   third

The Three Billy Goats Gruff

Circle the **third** picture.

Circle the **second** picture.

Circle the **first** picture.

Circle the **third** picture.

Think Back

Look at the pictures. Then, think back to the story "The Three Billy Goats Gruff." Circle all of the things you see that were in the story.

The Three Billy Goats Gruff

284   Comprehension/Story Details   Read and Learn With Classic Stories—Grade K

Big and Little

One Billy Goat Gruff was big and one was little. **Big** and **little** are opposites. Draw a line from a picture on the left to its opposite on the right.

The Three Billy Goats Gruff

What's Different?

Look at the two pictures below. There are four things in the second picture that are different from the first picture. Circle the things that are different.

Comprehension/Observing Details   Read and Learn With Classic Stories—Grade K

Find a Rhyme

Color the pictures in each row whose names rhyme.

Phonics/Rhyming

What Next?

The goats have had their fill of grass and are ready for some fun! Look at the goat in each box. Then, circle the picture that shows what you think the goat does next.

Comprehension/Making Predictions

Read and Learn With Classic Stories—Grade K

Small, Medium, or Large?

Cut out the pictures below. Sort them by size. Then, glue them in the correct place on page 291.

The Three Billy Goats Gruff

Small, Medium, or Large? (page 2)

Elizebeth

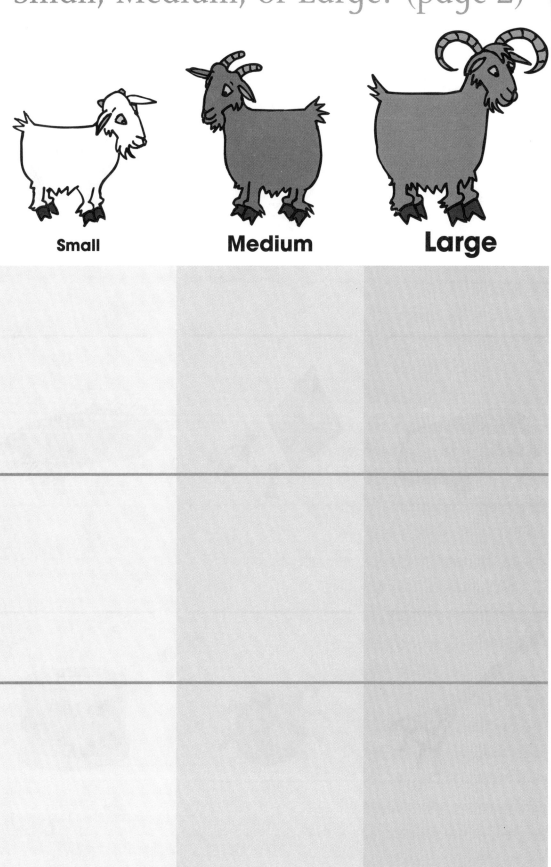

Small   **Medium**   **Large**

The Three Billy Goats Gruff

Gruff Says Short u

Gruff has the sound of **short u** in the middle. Say the
name of each picture. Write **u** on the line if the picture
name has the **short u** sound in the middle.

_____

_____

_____

U

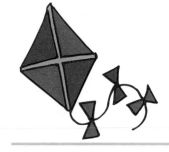

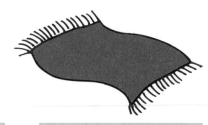

_____

_____

_____

_____

_____

_____

Words I Can Read

The words on the bridge are often used in stories. Read each word. Then, trace the words in this story.

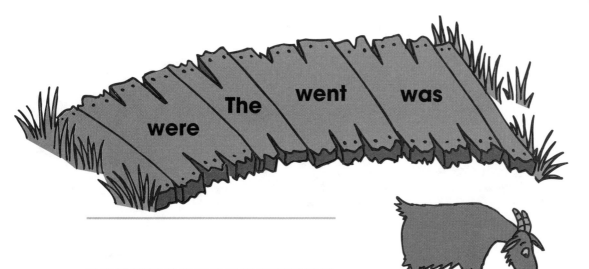

The Three Billy Goats Gruff

There __were__ three goats.

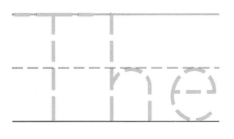

__The__ goats ate grass.

They __went__ to the river.

There __was__ a troll.

Pretend that the Three Billy Goats Gruff trip, trap, trip, trap up to your front door looking for something good to eat. What happens? Draw a picture about it. Then, tell a family member about your picture.

Reading Skills Checklist

Learning certain skills and strategies will help your child become a good reader. The following list shows the goals your child should reach in applying some basic skills during the kindergarten year. Use the checklist after reading each story to assess your child's reading progress. Choose only a handful of skills to check at any one time. Sample questions have been given for each skill.

Skill	Mother Goose Rhymes	Goldilocks and the Three Bears	The Gingerbread Man	Little Red Riding Hood	The Three Little Pigs	The Three Billy Goats Gruff
Cause and Effect Child recognizes that some actions or events can cause other events or results to happen. *Why did the kittens' mother say they could have no pie?* *What made the billy goats decide to cross the river?*						
Classify/Categorize Child can sort similar things into groups. *How are these things alike?* *Which things don't belong in this group?*						
Compare and Contrast Child can tell how two things are the same and how they are different. *How are the little pigs the same? How were the houses they built different?*						
Draw Conclusions Child can use information from a story and from real life to draw conclusions that are not stated in the story. *Why do you think Goldilocks went into the bears' house?*						
Main Idea Child can tell what a story is about. *What is this story mainly about?*						
Phonics Child can identify the letters of the alphabet and can tell which letters stand for some sounds, especially consonants. *What letter stands for the sound you hear at the beginning of* red?						
Picture Clues Child can use illustrations to help identify words in a story. *What is happening in this picture?*						
Predict Outcomes Child can tell what might happen next in a story. The prediction need not be accurate, as long as it is generally consistent with what has happened so far in the story. (during reading) *What do you think will happen next in the story?* (after reading on) *Did your prediction match what really happened?*						

Skill	Mother Goose Rhymes	Goldilocks and the Three Bears	The Gingerbread Man	Little Red Riding Hood	The Three Little Pigs	The Three Billy Goats Gruff
Reality/Fantasy Child can tell whether a story could happen in real life or is make-believe, and can support the answer with a reason. *What can really happen in this story? Why do you think so? What is make-believe? Why do you think so?*						
Retell a Story Child can retell major events in a story in his or her own words. *What happened in this story?*						
Sequence Child can tell what happens **first, next,** and **last** in a story. *What happened first? after that? last?*						
Character Child can identify people or animals in a story and can discuss their feelings and actions. *Who is in this story? Who made a gingerbread man? Why did she do that?*						

Answer Key

211

A Tall Wall

Look! Humpty Dumpty is sitting on a tall wall. Let's hope he doesn't fall! Look at all of the pictures on the wall. Draw a line to connect the pictures with rhyming names.

213

J Is for Jack and Jill

Jack and **Jill** both have names that begin with the sound of **j**. Look at the pictures. Write **j** on the line if the picture name begins with the sound of **j**.

214

Shoes for This and That

Do you remember the old woman who lived in a shoe? There are many different kinds of shoes. Draw a line to match each shoe with its activity.

215

Shell for Short e

Shell has the sound of **short e**. Circle the things in the pumpkin shell that have the sound of **short e**.

216

Sky High

What do you see when you look up in the sky? Color each thing that you might see in the sky.

217

What Color Is It?

Read the color words in the list. Then, color each animal the correct color.

black   brown   blue   green

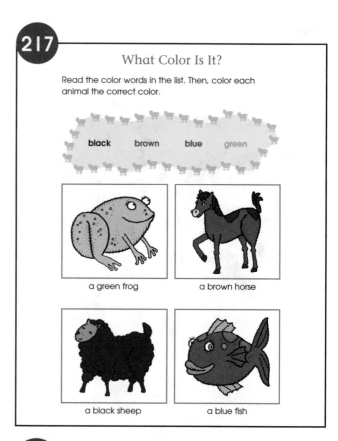

a green frog

a brown horse

a black sheep

a blue fish

218

The Dish Ran Away With the Spoon

Dish has the sound of **short i**. Say the name of each picture. Circle each picture whose name has the **short i** sound.

219

Going Shopping

Here are some things you may find when you go the market, or grocery store. Draw a line to match the picture with its name.

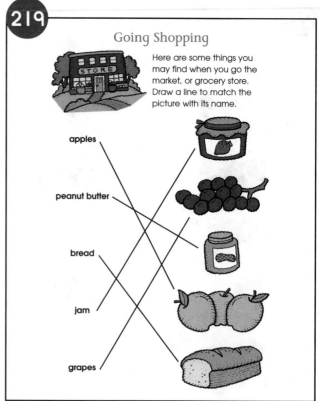

apples

peanut butter

bread

jam

grapes

220

School Days

Mary's lamb can't really read a book in school! Look at the pictures. Put an **X** on the pictures that show something that could **not** really happen in school.

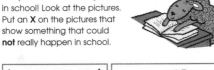

221

Teddy Bear Time

It's time to finish the picture of the teddy bear. Follow the directions.

1. Draw a  on the teddy bear.

2. Color his  blue.

3. Draw a  on his face.

4. Color his  red.

222

What Goes In It?

Draw lines from the pie to each thing that you could bake in a pie. Then, draw lines from the garden to each thing you could grow in a garden.

223

Number Match-Up

Say the rhyme "One, Two, Buckle My Shoe." As you say the words, circle the picture that goes with each set of numbers.

1, 2, . . .

3, 4, . . .

5, 6, . . .

7, 8, . . .

9, 10, . . .

224

Lost!

Help the kittens find their lost mittens! Connect the pictures whose names begin with the sound of **l**.

227

What Happens Next?

Cut out the pictures below. Put them in the order they happened in the story. Then, glue the pictures in the correct order onto another sheet of paper.

229

How Do They Feel?

Look at the pictures below. Color the face that shows how each character feels.

230

Meet My Family

The family of the Three Bears includes Baby Bear, Mama Bear, and Papa Bear. Who is in your family? Draw your family in the box below. Show your family members in order from smallest to largest.

Answers will vary.

231

Rhyme Time

Goldilocks and Baby Bear are playing a rhyming game together. Cut out the picture cards. Then, match the pictures whose names rhyme. Say the rhyming words.

233

B Is for Bear

Bear begins with the sound of **b**. Color the pictures whose names begin with the **b** sound.

234

What Does Not Belong?

Goldilocks does not belong with Baby Bear, Mama Bear, and Papa Bear. Look at the pictures below. Draw an **X** on the picture in each row that **does not** belong.

235

What's Cooking?

What will the Three Bears cook up next? Look at the ingredients in each box. Then, color the food you think the Three Bears will make.

236

G Is for Goldilocks

Goldilocks begins with the sound of **g**. Write **g** next to each picture whose name begins with the **g** sound.

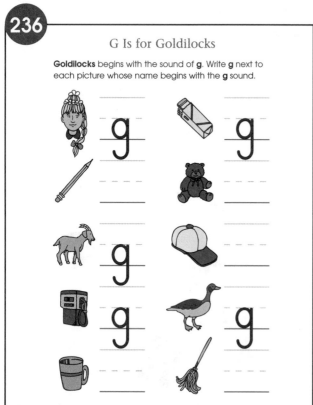

237

Hot and Cold

Words like **hot** and **cold** are called **opposites**. Circle the two pictures in each row that show opposites.

238

Hello, Neighbor!

What do you think would happen if the Three Bears came to Goldilocks' house? Tell what you think would happen. Then, draw a picture to show it.

Answers will vary.

239

Who Was First?

Cut out the pictures of the characters below. Glue them in the order that the Gingerbread Man met them.

241

We Go Together

Look at the pictures in each row, and circle the two that go together. Then, tell why they go together.

242

My Favorite Part

What is your favorite part of the story? Draw a picture showing it. Tell someone else about your picture.

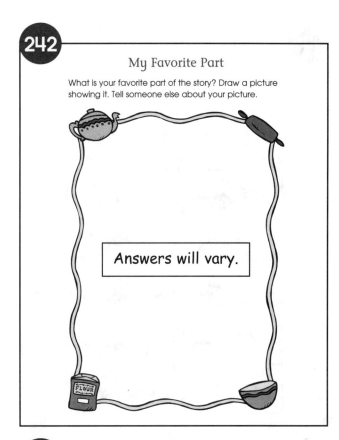

Answers will vary.

243

M Is for Man

Man begins with the sound of **m**. Color the space red if the name of the picture in it begins with the **m** sound. What letter do you see?

244

Listen for Short a

Cat has the **short a** sound. Print **a** on the line if the picture name has the **short a** sound.

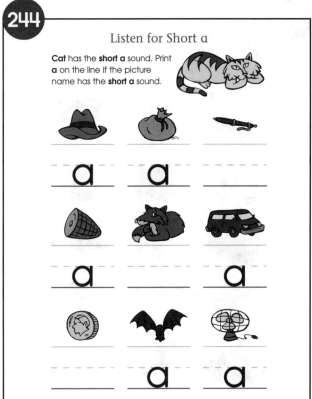

245

Rhyme Time Game

Play this rhyming game with a friend.

How to play:
1. Cut out the cards. Mix them up and put them facedown.
2. Take turns turning over two cards. If they rhyme, keep them. If they do not, put them back.
3. Keep playing until all the cards have been used.

247

Could It Really Happen?

It's fun to make believe that a gingerbread man can run fast, isn't it? But a gingerbread man really can't run at all. Color the pictures that show things that could really happen.

249

Gingerbread Cookies

Making gingerbread cookies sure is fun! Circle the picture in each row that shows something you use to make gingerbread cookies.

250

Listen for Short o

Fox has the **short o** sound. Color the pictures whose names have the **short o** sound.

251

As Fast As You Can!

In the story, the Gingerbread Man was **fast**. Put an **X** on the picture in each box that shows something that moves **fast**.

252

A New Ending

How else could the story of "The Gingerbread Man" have ended? Draw a new ending to the story. Tell about your new ending.

Answers will vary.

253

My Own Storybook

Cut out the pictures. Put them in the correct order to tell the story. Then, make your own storybook.

255

Real or Make-Believe?

Look at the pictures. Circle each picture that shows something real. Put an **X** on each picture that shows something make-believe.

256

Which One Is Different?

Look at the pictures in each row. Circle the one that is different. Tell how it is different.

257

It Begins With H

Hood begins with the sound of **h**. Help Little Red Riding Hood look for things that begin with the sound of **h**. Circle those things in the picture.

258

Let's Have a Picnic!

Go on a picnic with Little Red Riding Hood. Which things will you need for your picnic? Draw a line from each thing you will need to the picnic blanket.

259

W Is for Wolf

Wolf begins with the sound of **w**. Go shopping with the wolf. Color all of the things in the store that begin with the sound of **w**.

260

A Picture of Grandmother

Finish this picture of Little Red Riding Hood's grandmother. Give her **eyes, ears, hands,** and **teeth**. Talk about what each body part is used for. Then, draw a line from the word to the body part.

261

Match Up

Cut out the picture cards and word cards below and on page 263. Mix up the cards. Put them faceup on a table. Match each word or name with its picture.

263

Match Up (page 2)

265

Going to Grandma's House

Little Red Riding Hood is going to Grandmother's house. Which is the shorter path? Color that path **blue**. Color the longer path **orange**. Color the trees **green** and **brown**. Color the flowers **red**.

266

A Special Time

Draw a picture about a special time you had with a grandparent or other family member. Show your drawing and tell about it. Then, write some words or a sentence about it.

Answers will vary.

271

One, Two, Three

Words can stand for numbers. Look at each picture, and write the correct number word on the line.

one   two   three

one   two

three   two

one   three

272

Home, Sweet Home

The Three Little Pigs made their homes from different things. Circle the homes that were built with the same things that the pigs used.

273

Two of a Kind

Look at the pictures in each row. Circle the two pictures that are alike in some way. Then, tell why they are alike.

274

It's a Party!

The Three Little Pigs are so glad the wolf is gone that they are going to have a big party. Look at the party items in each box. Put an **X** on the item that is different in some way. Then, tell how it is different.

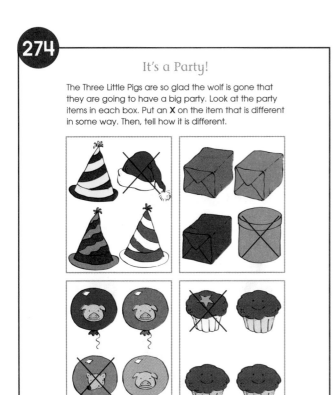

275

Tell the Order

Think about the story. Write the numbers 1, 2, 3, and 4 in the boxes to show the correct order.

276

Which One Doesn't Belong?

The wolf does not belong with the Three Little Pigs. Draw an **X** on the picture that **does not** belong in each row. Then, tell why it doesn't belong.

277

What Rhymes With Pig?

Look at the pictures. Which ones rhyme with pig? Trace the words that rhyme with pig.

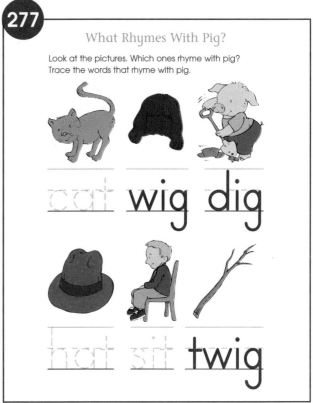

cat wig dig

hat sit twig

278

Pig Begins With P

Pig begins with the sound of **p**. Look at the picture of the Three Little Pigs' picnic in the park. Color all the things that begin with the sound of **p**.

279

Pig Ends With G

Pig begins with **p** but it ends with **g**. Say the name of each picture. Listen for the ending sound. Color the pictures whose names end with the sound of **g**.

280

And Then . . .

Draw a picture about what you think the Three Little Pigs did after the wolf ran away. Tell about your picture.

Answers will vary.

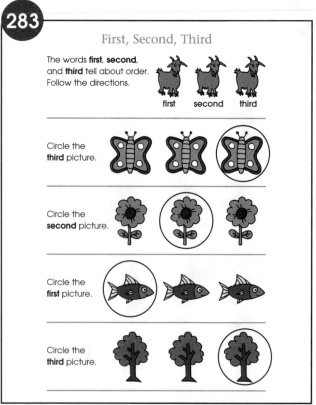

283

First, Second, Third

The words **first**, **second**, and **third** tell about order. Follow the directions.

first   second   third

Circle the **third** picture.

Circle the **second** picture.

Circle the **first** picture.

Circle the **third** picture.

284

Think Back

Look at the pictures. Then, think back to the story "The Three Billy Goats Gruff." Circle all of the things you see that were in the story.

285

Big and Little

One Billy Goat Gruff was big and one was little. **Big** and **little** are opposites. Draw a line from a picture on the left to its opposite on the right.

286

What's Different?

Look at the two pictures below. There are four things in the second picture that are different from the first picture. Circle the things that are different.

287

Find a Rhyme

Color the pictures in each row whose names rhyme.

288

What Next?

The goats have had their fill of grass and are ready for some fun! Look at the goat in each box. Then, circle the picture that shows what you think the goat does next.

291

Small, Medium, or Large? (page 2)

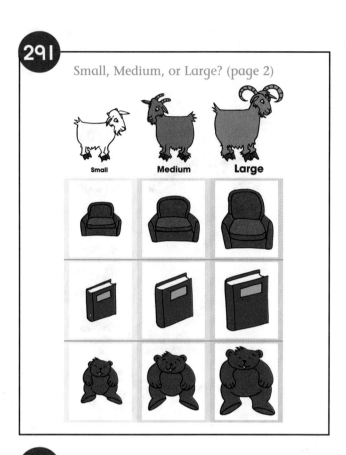

292

Gruff Says Short u

Gruff has the sound of **short u** in the middle. Say the name of each picture. Write **u** on the line if the picture name has the **short u** sound in the middle.

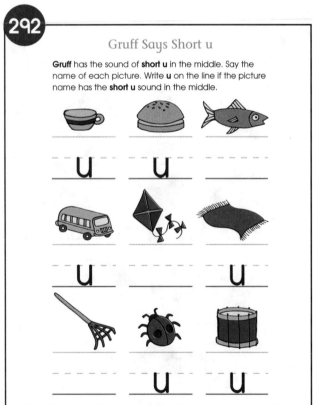

293

Words I Can Read

The words on the bridge are often used in stories. Read each word. Then, trace the words in this story.

A Visit from the
Three Billy Goats Gruff

Pretend that the Three Billy Goats Gruff trip, trap, trip, trap up to your front door looking for something good to eat. What happens? Draw a picture about it. Then, tell a family member about your picture.

Answers will vary.

Everyday Learning Activities

Learning can become an everyday experience for your child. The activities on the following pages can act as a springboard for learning. Some of the suggested activities are structured and require readily available materials. Others may be used spontaneously as you are driving, shopping, or engaging in other everyday activities. The activities are arranged according to subject areas.

Reading Readiness

Words All Around When riding in a car, walking down the street, or shopping in a mall, point out signs such as STOP, EXIT, names of stores, and so on. Read the words and have your child repeat them after you. Talk about what each sign means. Soon your child will be reading them independently.

Kitchen Phonics Post magnetic letters of the alphabet on the refrigerator. When you are putting grocery items away or taking them out, say, "*M* is for mushroom. Can you find an *m*?" or "*A* is for apple. Where is the *a*?"

Describing Words Choose an object in the room, or nearby if you're outside, and describe it with two adjectives. Say, for example, "Can you find something huge and lumpy?" If your child makes an incorrect guess, add another adjective. For example, "The thing is huge, lumpy, and broken." Words describing color, size, shape, texture, and other attributes are useful. Continue until your child guesses the object. Then have him or her choose an object and give you clues. You might occasionally make silly guesses to give your child more practice.

Reading Along As you read a familiar book that has repetitive or rhyming text, such as *Brown Bear, Brown Bear, What Do You See?*, pause before the end of each sentence and let your child say the missing word. Encourage your child to chime in with you as you read the story.

Previewing a Book Before reading a book aloud to your child, read the title and the author's name. Then, together, look at a few of the pictures (without giving away the ending), and have your child tell you what is happening in the illustrations. Before you begin reading, encourage your child to tell what he or she thinks the story will be about.

Making Predictions As you read aloud together, encourage your child to predict what he or she thinks will happen next in the story. After you turn the page, look at the picture and check the prediction. Your child can then change or confirm the prediction. Making predictions should be fun, with a goal of making a logical guess as to what will happen next.

3-D Letters As your child is learning the letters of the alphabet, help him or her use clay or modeling dough to form the letters. Glue each letter on a sheet of construction paper and let your child feel the shape. You may also choose to make tactile letters out of chenille stems (pipe cleaners), cotton balls, or yarn.

Begins Like . . . Gather eight to ten toys or other objects whose names begin with different consonant sounds, and put them on a table. Ask your child to point to the one that begins with a certain sound. For example, if you say, "What begins with *p* like *pencil?*" your child would point to the pinwheel.

Sorting Like Things Gather like objects, such as writing objects, cooking objects, paper products, and toys, on a table. Choose three like objects and one that does not belong to the group (for example, pencil, crayon, pen, spoon). Let your child choose the one that does not belong.

Opposites Work with your child to name words that are opposite in meaning. Point to something that is little, and then have your child find something big. Continue with other antonyms such as *sweet/sour, strong/weak, happy/sad.*

Feelings Look through a book, a magazine, or the comics with your child. Ask how a character is feeling. Read part of the material aloud, and ask your child why the character is feeling that way. Encourage your child to tell about a time he or she felt that way.

Color Words Write a color word on a piece of paper. Then look together in a magazine to find pictures of objects that are that color. Your child can cut out the pictures and glue them to the paper.

Word Labels You may wish to label different items in your child's bedroom or other rooms in your home with written labels, such as *table, chair, door, window,* and *toy chest.* Have your child "read" the labels from time to time.

Missing Sound With your child, look at a favorite illustrated storybook. Say the name of an object or character in a picture, leaving out the beginning sound. For example, if you saw a *cow,* you would say *ow.* Have your child say the complete word.

Library Books Try to go to the library with your child at least once a week. Choose one or two books that have a lot of repetition, such as *Whose Cat Is This?* or *I Went Walking*. Let your child choose another book or two. Encourage him or her to tell you why he or she thinks those books will be good. Read the books several times together during the week.

I Spy Instead of using colors in the game "I Spy," use beginning sounds or rhymes. For example, say "I spy something that begins like *hat*" or "I spy something that rhymes with *mouse*." Have your child guess the object's name.

Giving a Present Write on an index card a word you think your child would like to know, such as *rainbow*, *elephant*, *rhinoceros*, or *dinosaur*. Decorate the card with a picture. Wrap up the word as if it were a gift, and give it to your child. When your child opens it, say the word together and use it in a sentence. Let your child put the gift in a special place. Repeat as often as your child remains interested.

Beanbag Toss Draw a large grid on a piece of paper or posterboard, and write a different lowercase consonant in each box on the grid. Then, have your child toss a beanbag on the paper. Have him or her say the letter the beanbag lands on and suggest a word that begins with that letter. You might want to keep score, letting your child score one point for each word named.

Memory Game Show your child a family photograph. Look together at it and discuss what you see. Then, remove the photograph. Make a game of asking your child questions about the photo, such as who is in it, where the picture was taken, what color Mom's dress is, and so on. Show the photograph again and let your child find the answers he or she could not remember.

Matching Words Make word cards by cutting a few 8 x 11 inch sheets of paper into four strips or by cutting large index cards in half. Draw a line down the middle of each card. Then, write a word on each side of the line. Use word pairs such as the ones shown here. Show your child each card and ask whether the words are the same or different. If necessary, help him or her find the differences between word pairs that are different. If your child wants to read the words, provide assistance as needed.

fan	fun		was	saw		bat	bag		log	log		ant	tan		hat	hat

Paper Bag Puppets After you read a story, let your child choose a favorite character. Your child can make a puppet with a small paper bag, markers, construction paper, scissors, glue, and other art materials. Then, let your child use the puppet and retell part of the story.

Mathematics

Sorting and Counting Fill a small bowl with different kinds of small dry foods, such as pasta bow ties, dried beans, and nuts in the shell. Have your child sort them into different groups. Then, have him or her count the number of items in each group.

Making a Counting Book Use twenty sheets of clean paper, and write the numerals 1–20, one on each page. Then, work with your child to illustrate each number with that many objects. You can draw six dots, find pictures of three children, glue on four cotton balls or two buttons, and so on. Bind together the pages to make a counting book by stapling it or by punching holes in the left margin and tying a length of yarn through the holes.

Dominoes Play dominoes with your child. He or she can match numbers and count the dots on each domino. After playing, count the total dominoes used in the game.

Which Is Bigger? Point to two similar objects and ask, "Which is bigger?" Then gather small groups of like objects, such as toy animals, and have your child arrange the objects from smallest to biggest.

Matching Shapes Cut out different sizes of circles, triangles, squares, and rectangles from different colors of construction paper. Then, have your child find the circles, the triangles, the squares, and the rectangles. Next, ask him or her to find specific shapes, for example, "Find the green triangle." Your child can also sort the shapes according to like color or size. After sorting, let your child arrange the shapes into a picture and glue them onto a piece of white paper.

Calendar Help your child make a calendar for the month on a large sheet of paper. Help him or her write the days of the week and then fill in the numbers on the appropriate days. You also may wish to post your child's appointments, family birthdays, and other special events, using pictures and words.

Science

Nature Walk During a walk through a park, point out different animals. Discuss with your child any facts you know about what the animal eats, where it stays during the winter months, and any other habits of that animal.

Walking Like an Animal Encourage your child to watch how an animal moves from place to place. Your child will also enjoy moving like the animal he or she sees. For example, your child can slink like a cat, pounce like a puppy, bob his or her head like a walking pigeon, or gallop like a horse.

Pond Fun On a trip to a pond, gather a light-colored bucket full of pond water. Use a net to scoop up swimmers, dragonflies, water beetles, or pollywogs and place them in the bucket. Have your child watch the different animals to see what they look like and how they swim. If your child wants to hold the animal, gather it up inside a clear plastic bag so it doesn't get crushed. After looking at the animals, return them to their pond.

Treasure Bag As you walk along a trail in the woods or park or on a beach, without picking growing things, let your child gather natural treasures such as interesting rocks, shells, fallen blossoms, seeds, and soft colorful leaves. When one object is found, encourage your child to find a matching object. When you finish your walk, have your child describe each treasure he or she found. You may want to have your child return the treasures back to nature.

Tree Detectives Have your child choose a favorite tree. Then, be tree detectives together. Take time to observe the tree. Check the tree trunk, looking for holes that insects and birds have made. Using a magnifying glass, look for ants, spiders, or beetles. Scan the trunk to see if there are any scratches that might have been made by mice, squirrels, chipmunks, raccoons, foxes, lizards, or tree frogs. Listen for sounds that tell you animals are in the tree now. If you have a stethoscope, listen to the tree's trunk and see if you can hear sap rushing inside. Look up in the tree for birds' nests, beehives, or spiderwebs. Help your child make a list of everything you observe together.

Social Studies

Getting There Talk with your child about different ways to get to school, to a grandparent's house, to a beach, and to other places near and far. Work with your child to make a book called "Ways to Travel," drawing and labeling each mode of transportation.

Mapping It Out Your child can make a map of a favorite walking trail or route to school. He or she can begin by making a dot where the path begins and an X on the other side of the page. As you walk along the trail, stop from time to time, so your child can draw buildings or other places of interest between the two points.

Jobs Around Town Talk with your child about the different jobs people have in the community. Name the job and then discuss what is involved in that person's job. Discuss how that job helps people in your neighborhood or town. Then, discuss ways family members help one another at home.

Field Trips Take your child to different business establishments or community facilities, such as a bakery, a grocery store, a fire station, or a police station. Try to go at a time that is not usually very busy. If possible, ask a store manager to find a professional in the store who can show and tell what he or she does for a living.

Making a 3-D Map Draw on a large sheet of paper or posterboard the streets in and around your neighborhood. Gather materials such as markers, shoe boxes, gift boxes, glue, and natural materials. Help your child use the materials to place and decorate buildings, parks, houses and other sites that belong in your neighborhood. Encourage him or her to move a toy car along the roads to go from place to place.

Fitness and Movement

Throwing a Ball Practice throwing, catching, and kicking different kinds of balls with your child. Make the activity fun, not a competition. This practice can help develop your child's overall physical coordination.

Obstacle Course Set up an obstacle course for your child to run through. You can use a small barrier (no higher than 6 inches) for jumping, a plastic tunnel for crawling through, and large objects for running around.

Pigs to Market Give your child a driving stick (a broomstick, a yardstick, or a dowel about three feet long) and place a plastic two-liter bottle (the pig) on the ground. Designate a starting line and a goal (the market). Have your child drive the pig to market and back by pushing the bottle with the stick. For a bit of light-hearted self-competition, you might time your child driving the pig to market and back and then challenge him or her to do it again, trying to beat the time of the first attempt.

Lacing Cards Your child can practice lacing with lacing cards made from cardboard and shoelaces. Punch holes along the outside of a cardboard design, tie the shoelace to one end of the card, and let your child lace up, following the outline of the design.

Amazing Mazes Draw simple mazes for your child to follow with a crayon. Following mazes is particularly good for eye-hand coordination. Be sure your maze goes from left to right and top to bottom, to help your child get used to the directions he or she will follow in reading.